KANGAROO

LIFE CYCLES

Words that look like **this** can be found in the glossary on page 24.

BookLife PUBLISHING

©2019
BookLife Publishing Ltd.
King's Lynn
Norfolk PE30 4LS

All rights reserved. Printed in Malaysia.

A catalogue record for this book is available from the British Library.

ISBN: 978-1-78637-732-6

Written by:
Shalini Vallepur

Edited by:
William Anthony

Designed by:
Danielle Jones

All facts, statistics, web addresses and URLs in this book were verified as valid and accurate at time of writing. No responsibility for any changes to external websites or references can be accepted by either the author or publisher.

CONTENTS

Page 4	**What Is a Life Cycle?**
Page 5	**What Is a Kangaroo?**
Page 6	**Newborn Joeys**
Page 10	**Joeys**
Page 12	**Kangaroos**
Page 14	**Kangaroo Life**
Page 16	**Types of Kangaroo**
Page 18	**Kangaroo Facts**
Page 20	**World Record Breakers**
Page 22	**Life Cycle of a Kangaroo**
Page 23	**Get Exploring!**
Page 24	**Glossary and Index**

WHAT IS A LIFE CYCLE?

All animals, plants and humans go through different stages of their life as they grow and change. This is called a life cycle.

Human life cycle

Baby → Child → Adult

WHAT IS A KANGAROO?

Kangaroos are a type of **marsupial**. They are **mammals** that live together in a group called a mob.

Female kangaroos carry their offspring in a pouch.

NEWBORN JOEYS

A female kangaroo is **pregnant** for around a month before she gives birth to a newborn joey. It can't see and it has no fur.

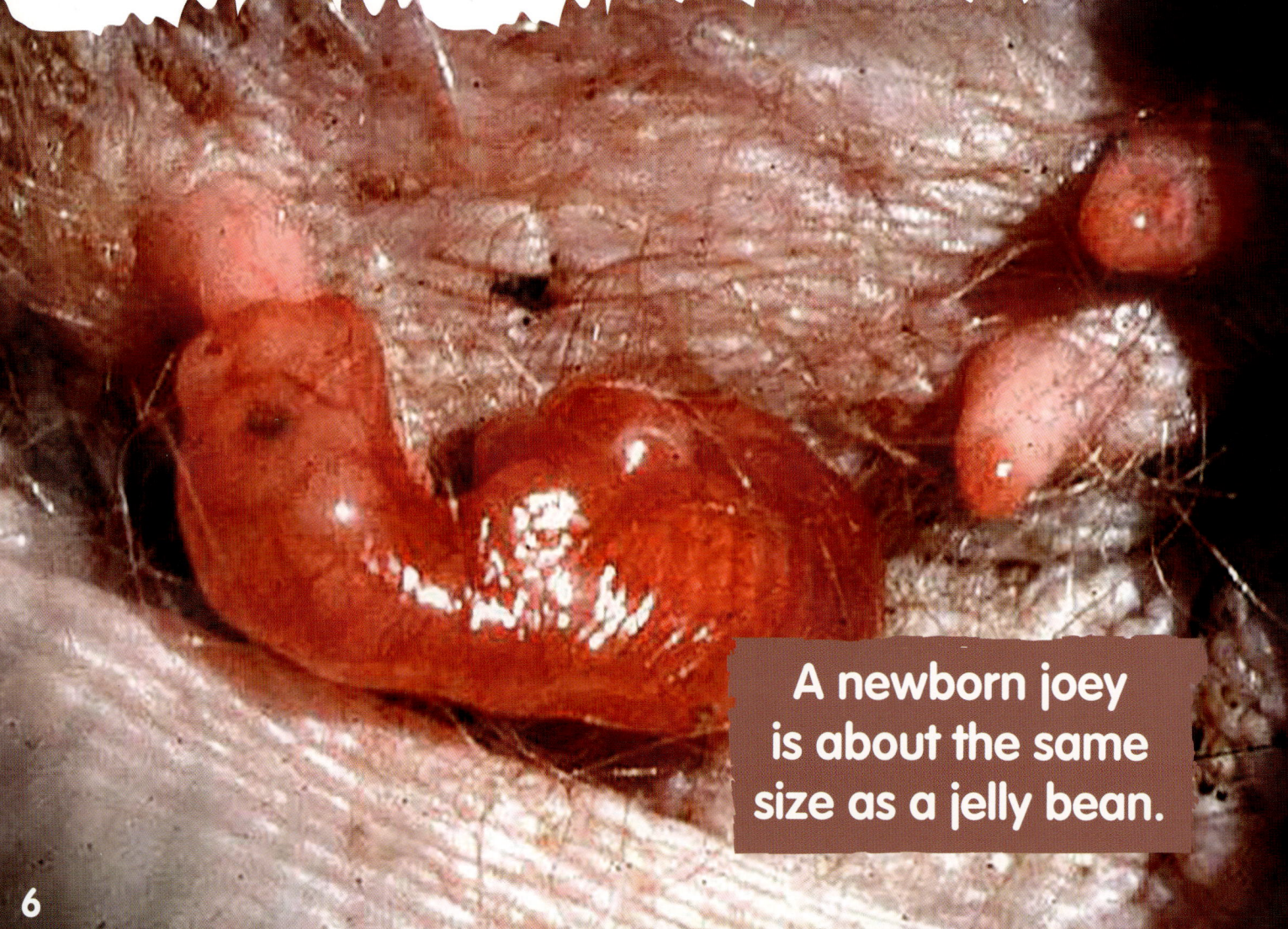

A newborn joey is about the same size as a jelly bean.

The newborn joey climbs towards its mother's pouch. The pouch is safe and warm. Once inside, the newborn keeps growing.

Can you see the pouch?

A newborn joey stays in the pouch and drinks milk from its mother. Drinking milk helps the newborn to grow.

This kangaroo has a full pouch. A joey must be inside.

The newborn joey can finally see and hear. It's time for it to take its first peek outside.

JOEYS

After around six months, the joey leaves its mother's pouch to explore. It never strays too far and can climb back into the pouch.

A joey keeps drinking its mother's milk to grow.

Joeys start eating grass just like adult kangaroos. At around ten months old, joeys are old enough to leave the pouch for good.

The joey joins the rest of the mob.

KANGAROOS

After between 14 months and 4 years, the joey will be a fully grown adult. Adult kangaroos will **mate** to start the life cycle again.

Male kangaroos will often fight over females. They use their arms and big legs to punch and kick each other. This is sometimes called boxing.

Their big tails are used for balance.

KANGAROO LIFE

Most kangaroos are crepuscular. This means they are active in the mornings and evenings. Kangaroos will rest in the shade during the day to stay cool.

It can get very hot during the day.

Kangaroos don't need to drink a lot of water. They get enough water from the food they eat. Kangaroos are **herbivores** that eat grass, shrubs and leaves.

TYPES OF KANGAROO

Kangaroos live in Australia. There are four different **species** of kangaroo. They are the red kangaroo, eastern grey kangaroo, western grey kangaroo and antilopine kangaroo.

Eastern grey kangaroos can weigh around 100 kilograms.

Eastern grey kangaroo

The antilopine kangaroo lives in the north of Australia, the hottest part. Males have red fur on their backs while females have grey.

KANGAROO FACTS

Instead of walking, kangaroos hop around. The **tendons** in a kangaroo's legs are like big springs that make hopping around easy.

Kangaroos live on land but they are very good swimmers. They may swim across water for food or if they are escaping from **predators**.

WORLD RECORD BREAKERS

Fastest Jumper

Red kangaroos can jump the fastest of the four kangaroo species. They can jump three metres high at speeds of up to 56 kilometres per hour!

Biggest Kangaroo

Red kangaroos are also the biggest species of kangaroo. The biggest ever recorded red kangaroo was 2.1 metres tall. That's taller than most adults.

LIFE CYCLE OF A KANGAROO

1 A female kangaroo gives birth.

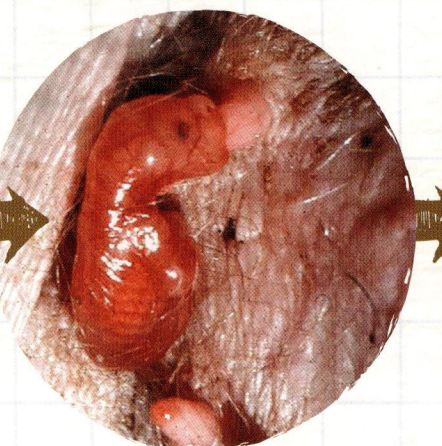

2 The newborn joey grows in the pouch.

3 The joey leaves the pouch and joins the mob.

4 The joey becomes an adult and finds a mate.

LIFE CYCLES

Get Exploring!

Do you want to learn more about kangaroos and joeys? Why not visit a zoo and see if there are any kangaroos?

GLOSSARY

herbivores	animals that only eat plants
mammals	animals that have warm blood, backbones and produce milk
marsupial	a type of mammal that looks after its young in its pouch
mate	a partner (of the same species) who an animal chooses to produce young with
offspring	the child or young of a living thing
predators	animals that hunt other animals for food
pregnant	when a mother develops a baby inside her
species	groups of very similar animals that are capable of producing young together
tendons	flexible cords that join muscles together

INDEX

Australia 16–17
females 5–6, 13, 17, 22
hop 18
joeys 6–12, 22–23
males 13, 17
milk 8, 10
mobs 5, 11, 22
newborns 6–9, 22
pouches 5, 7–8, 10–11, 22
red kangaroos 16–17, 20–21
swim 19
water 15, 19

PHOTO CREDITS

All images are courtesy of Shutterstock.com, unless otherwise specified. With thanks to Getty Images, Thinkstock Photo and iStockphoto. Front cover & 1 – Bradley Blackburn (kangaroo), ivleva1975 (doodles), Olga Tropinina (doodles). 2 – Andrea Izzotti. 3 – LifetimeStock, Natalia Fedosova, Bradley Blackburn. 4 – mimagephotography, zulufoto, Black-Photography, Julia Sanders. 5 – THPStock. 6 – Photograph by Geoff Shaw (Zoology, University of Melbourne, Australia). 7 – Michal Ninger. 8 – Mali lucky. 9 – K.A.Willis. 10 – Susan Flashman. 11 – A Pawel Papis. 12 – livcool. 13 – Breathes. 14 – RayPJ. 15 – Nuno Simoes. 16 – Alina Kurbiel. 17 – ChameleonsEye. 18 – LeonardF. 19 – worldswildlifewonders. 20 – Javid Kheyrabadi, Csdesign86. 21 – tynyuk, AnnstasAg, Migren art. 22 – Arun Sankaragal, ariff gizan, John Carnemolla, Susan Flashman. 23 – hedgehog94.